Raising
Adorable Children

Raising Adorable Children

Christian Parenting

Nancy Stanton Kempis

Copyright © 2018 by Nancy Stanton Kempis.

ISBN:	Softcover	978-1-9845-0999-4
	eBook	978-1-9845-1000-6

All rights reserved. No part of this book may be reproduced or transmitted in any form or by any means, electronic or mechanical, including photocopying, recording, or by any information storage and retrieval system, without permission in writing from the copyright owner.

KJV
Scripture quotations marked KJV are from the Holy Bible, King James Version (Authorized Version). First published in 1611. Quoted from the KJV Classic Reference Bible, Copyright © 1983 by The Zondervan Corporation

Any people depicted in stock imagery provided by Getty Images are models, and such images are being used for illustrative purposes only. Certain stock imagery © Getty Images.

Print information available on the last page.

Rev. date: 02/19/2018

To order additional copies of this book, contact:
Xlibris
1-888-795-4274
www.Xlibris.com
Orders@Xlibris.com
774264

Contents

Foreword ix

Chapter 1	Faith Begins at Home 1
Chapter 2	Training Begins at Conception 4
Chapter 3	Teaching a Newborn Baby 6
Chapter 4	Successful 0–18 Months 9
Chapter 5	Your Child's Emotional Development and You (Two to Seven Years) 11
Chapter 6	Christian Upbringing 14
Chapter 7	Teaching Obedience 16
Chapter 8	Why Obey? 18
Chapter 9	The Principle of God's Love 21
Chapter 10	Build Your Child for Greatness 23
Chapter 11	Framework for Healthy Habits 26
Chapter 12	Preteens' Challenges 29
Chapter 13	Developing Social Skills 32
Chapter 14	Cultivating Good Friendship Skills 35

This book is dedicated to the young parents of future generations of God-fearing, compassionate, and admirable children. It is my goal to share the Word of God as a guide for building up spiritually strong and happy individuals rooted in love, obedience, faith in God, and respect for others based on biblical principles.

To my four wonderful sons, who will be pillars of good moral values for the next generation of my bloodline, may these writings provide nuggets of wisdom for you and your chosen partners in life. Remember that the physical body of your child may come from you, but the spirit does not. Always seek the guidance of the Lord to give you wisdom and protection for the new soul that you are bringing out into this world. May this life that God entrusted in your care bring glory to Him and live a life according to His will and purpose.

FOREWORD

THE AUTHOR IS a dedicated member of our ministry since 2009. It is a great pleasure to see that through writing, Nancy desires to share her strong faith in the wisdom of the Word of God among the young couples and new mothers, who will bring forth the next generation. This book attempts to confront the rapidly deteriorating state of values and morality of the present generation by going back to its source. She writes from a mother's perspective with the inspiration of the Word of God.

Rev. Roel C. Tiongco
Senior pastor, Shalom Outreach Ministries, AG/NY

This book is a must for parents who would like to raise children to be happy, productive, well-adjusted, and purpose-driven individuals. This Christian writer, who has faced many insurmountable situations in her life, packed this book with wisdom from the Bible, psychological principles, and experiences of significant people in her life. A parenting book is made more interesting with her style of writing that deviates from the scholarly style that dominates the field. Nancy, who is truly a master of her domain, reaches to people of various walks of life and is successful in sending a general message that parenting, although challenging and frustrating at times, is a God-inspired task that has to be enjoyed to the fullest. This book is worth a full read.

Elvira P. Galang, EdD
Family and community education,
Teachers College, Columbia University, founder of LINGAP

CHAPTER 1

Faith Begins at Home

Train up the child in the way he should go and when he is old he will not depart from it.

–Proverbs 22:6

MY EARLY TRAINING from my mother, who was a devout Catholic, consisted of praying to God daily, saying grace before meals, and being grateful to God for every blessing that I received. In school, where catechism was taught, I learned the Ten Commandments, which I was told to follow as the guide in all my actions. I was told to fear God and avoid willfully committing sins that would surely send a person to hell.

Looking back, I realize that knowing about God is different from knowing God in a personal way. Knowing the commandments of God and the Golden Rule is not enough. I knew these by heart, but it did not help me achieve my goals and the things that my heart desired. In other words, I needed to grow spiritually, despite having head knowledge about everything I was taught as a child. What my mother and my early teachers did was only to sow a seed of faith in me from which I would grow and not depart from.

There is a famous saying that goes, "The hands that rock the cradle rule the world." We often overlook the deeper implication of this adage. The reality is that the child gets its training from the mother long before its birth. Its temperament and attitude is formed right from the time of inception. Parents who are happily looking forward to this child are already sowing the seed of self-confidence to the developing fetus. The feeling of joy is transmitted to the baby in the womb that as soon as that baby is born into the world, he or she has the innate capacity for joy and positive self-image. Compare this to a baby whose inception happened unexpectedly or one conceived accidentally (as in the case of single girls) and therefore must be kept hidden, shrouded in shame and regret. That baby comes out lacking in self-worth and, without subsequent proper nurturing, will show signs of unpleasant behavior.

Three years after I and my husband got married, I found out I was pregnant, and we were so delighted of his coming to our life despite the hardship we were going through at that time. When he was born, he was such a happy and peaceful bundle of joy that he was a delight to everyone who saw him. He smiled and giggled at a mere eye encounter or even slight attention he got from people. As such, he brought us too much blessings that extended even into our business and finances. We experienced tremendous growth in the succeeding years.

This made me very busy—so much so that when I conceived my second baby, I felt it was such a bad time to be pregnant. My business was at its pinnacle, and I was uneasy and did not feel excited about another baby coming. I felt stressed and had a bad temper. When my baby was born, I was surprised at how he looked so unhappy. He frowned all the time and was not welcoming of any attention at all. He seemed annoyed at any kind of sound that my home was kept in complete silence all day long that you could hear a pin drop. It was my mother-in-law who explained to me why my baby displayed such a kind of attitude and traced it back to the time I was conceiving. Since then, I became careful and mindful how I acted toward my children from the moment I knew I had them in my womb.

The Bible is filled with instructions on how to raise successful children. As a responsible Christian mother, it is our ultimate responsibility to mold our children to become delightful and upright individuals raised with the right beliefs and principles based on the Word of God. We love, nurture, and cherish that child until he is grown-up. In the process, we teach him by what he sees in us more than what he hears from us. He watches how we deal with life and how we live it, and he learns by the example that we show him every moment of his growing years. He inherits our character more than our looks. He becomes a reflection of our character. The parents impart beliefs, attitudes, and emotions. Unless we have them right and live rightly, we cannot expect anything different from our children.

Basically, as we are molding the little children in the way they should go, we must learn to smile to teach them to smile and be happy and become positive individuals. We must acknowledge their worth to make them feel worthy. Our words are powerful, so we must prophesy only good things. Tell the child every positive affirmation. Say "You are blessed," and he will think, *I am blessed.* Say "You are smart" or "You are beautiful" or "You are not ordinary" or "You are a child of God." The child will begin to acknowledge and affirm to himself or herself the power of "I Am." His thoughts will be filled with self-esteem-enhancing thoughts. *I am blessed. I am smart. I am not ordinary. I am the child of the Most High God.* Hug them as often as possible to make them feel loved, and speak warm words that they may know they are cherished. Give them complete attention whenever they ask for it. In other words, wrap them with your love, and they will grow up a confident and loving person.

There are opposing opinions about the Word of God as written in Proverbs 13:24, which says, "Those who spares the rod of discipline hates his son, but he who loves him is careful to discipline him." This verse tells us that as parents, we have the responsibility to lead our children to Christ and discipline is critical in this process. On the other hand, a child who feels rejection will learn to fight, and a child who is constantly ignored will lose self-confidence and become frustrated. These negative feelings will ultimately surface in the form of rebellious attitude. Parents cannot, in any way, blame other people and outside circumstances for the change in the child's behavior, but rather, parents must examine how the child developed such changes and should promptly make careful adjustments and go back to the basics. Kids are kids all over the world, no matter what culture or religion. They can only learn from what they see and observe from us parents.

The Bible says in Matthew 5:14, "You are the light of the world. A city on a hill cannot be hidden." Parents must be the beacon of light in their household. Be the light that will train up the child in the way he should go. Help them learn to be resourceful, to be self-reliant, and to think independently. Teach them how to survive and thrive in this world and that they have the ability to choose what is right. Since salvation is the most important choice a person will ever make, the child should understand that there is a consequence of sin and that we are accountable for our actions.

At an early age, when God is understood mainly as a loving father in heaven, the question is not how the child will learn about God but from whom the child can learn about God. If we do not teach them at home, the world will teach them.

CHAPTER 2

Training Begins at Conception

I AM BLESSED TO have been able to study about child development during my early years in college. The knowledge that I got helped me at the time I became a mother of four highly energetic boys. With the help of my mother-in-law, who contributed some of her wisdom in childbearing and child-rearing, I consider myself blessed indeed. Everything that I have learned, including the hands-on experience I had in raising my own four boys, also led me to successfully assist in training candidates for newborn baby specialists while managing a baby-nursing agency, Neonate Care Agency, in New York City.

Mothers carry their baby in their womb for nine months, during which emotions and impulses are constantly transmitted to this new soul that we are bringing into the world. From the moment the mother begins planning to have a child, how she feels during that time is very important to the well-being of her baby. Mothers should meditate on the grace of God to have the strength to nourish the child and appreciate God for the gift of a developing soul. Be happy.

> May the words of my mouth and the meditation of my heart be pleasing in your sight, Oh Lord, my Rock and my Redeemer. (Psalm 19:14)

Being a parent should be a joyous experience. Parents, being the child's first teachers, should have strong spiritual convictions, and a mother should begin to include the child in her womb in her worship. Since no one can fully understand God by their own power unless they are devoted to God, the expectant mother should increase her devotion. Beginning at the time of conception, the bond between the mother and the child already starts to develop, and also, the environment of worship must be established. Keep in mind that the child's body comes from you, but the spirit does not.

It is written in the book of Jeremiah 1:5, "Before I formed you in the womb I knew you, before you were born I set you apart. Psalm 139:13 says, "For you created my inmost being, you knit me together in my mother's womb." Therefore, we know that the child we carry is God's creation, and as parents, we must assume the duty of calling upon God to bless and protect the child entrusted in our care. We are responsible for the nurturing of his body and soul.

Forty weeks of gestation can be a challenging time, even for the happy and expectant mother. Mothers go through varied emotions toward the approaching childbirth. Events such as baby shower parties should not be about gifts alone, but it should be a blessing ritual for both the mother and child. Baby showers must be a time our spirits should be nourished by those around us, our friends and relatives. This time has a special value in giving a new mother encouragement and support to banish her fears and give her strength through prayers. This is a unique occasion the mother could look forward to while waiting for the day of giving birth. The book of Psalms offers a lot of encouraging verses. Below, just to name a few, are some that the mother can meditate on.

> God is our refuge and strength, an ever present help in trouble.
> (Psalms 46:1)

And in verse 10, it says, "Be still and know that I am God."

> The Lord is my strength and my song; he has become my salvation.
> (Psalm 118:14)

Our parents may have told us that a woman giving birth has one foot in the grave, but I say that in that very moment of birthing, we have walked through the valley of the shadow of death. And as soon as the child is born, we have been delivered. God is with us in the mystery of procreation; therefore, we must put all our trust in Him. He tells us to be still and know that He is God.

CHAPTER 3

Teaching a Newborn Baby

Jesus said, "My grace is sufficient for you, for my power is made perfect in weakness."

–2 Corinthians 12:9

HOW PREPARED ARE you as parents to handle this great responsibility? You must have an understanding of the stages of development of the newborn baby in order to be successful in this most important undertaking in your life as a couple. Teaching a child is truly a joyous experience for both parents, but the mother has the primary responsibility during the initial days of the arrival of her baby into this world.

For the past nine months, the baby curled in the security of the womb; and at the moment of birth, this baby just went through a traumatic experience. The baby lets out a cry upon arrival into this new unfamiliar environment, and we usually miss the subtle miracles that occur in that very moment. The baby takes in his first breath of life and finds his voice for the very first time.

There is a medical reason why the newborn must cry during that first twenty seconds of birth, but that first cry brings miraculous, instant healing to the mother who, just moments ago, went through shivering pain we call the pangs of childbirth. The baby is alive, and that excruciating experience instantly vanishes and turns into gladness and an enormous sense of gratitude that they both got delivered safely.

We celebrate this new life, and this is clearly evident in how we almost immediately turn all our attention to the needs of the newborn. The mother miraculously forgets her travails and would want to wrap her baby to provide a similar sense of security in the womb. At this point, most mothers may decide to breastfeed her baby to provide the best nourishment that, healthwise, benefits both the giver and the receiver. As the feeding flows from mother to child, a new level of bond is created. Breastfeeding becomes a ritual during which the baby develops trust in his mother before anybody else, and he begins to adjust to his new environment and adopts into the new way of feeding. It is during this complete and exclusive attention during breastfeeding that the baby learns the warm, intimate, and caring relationship that bonds him to his mother.

It is also important to note that at the time the baby is born, he is not yet fully developed. A more noticeable outward sign is his limited range of eyesight. During the first four weeks, the newborn is merely continuing the development of his senses and other bodily functions while recovering his birth weight. He sees only within a twelve-inch range. At this stage, the newborn begins to explore the world through his senses according to his surrounding. The sound of people, the music, the light, the temperature, and even the voice, the touch, and the smell of the mother are factors to the child's learning and development.

Sometimes, mothers face challenges during the first few weeks of birth. There is the delicate umbilical cord and, if it's a boy, circumcision that needs extreme care within the first week. Some babies have acid reflux, and a pediatrician's advice is needed. Some are colicky, and the new mother becomes frustrated about what to do to appease the baby that keeps crying without apparent reason. We should understand that this baby will just overcome it by four to six weeks and settle down. Mothers should learn to differentiate the baby's cry. It could only be that the baby is uncomfortable, hungry, or sometimes tired; and once the need is met, the baby simply settles down.

In the succeeding four weeks, the baby, with proper guidance, begins to learn the difference between day and night. While this training is undertaken, parents should incorporate their spiritual practices into the baby's daily schedule to set the tone for the child's spiritual upbringing.

> Train up the child in the way he should go and when he is old he will not depart from it. (Proverbs 22:6)

As the baby makes progress, there is a sense of wonderment in witnessing as the baby starts rooting as it responds to movements around the room. You, as a parent, should enjoy the realization that the baby's eyesight is already developing and, soon, he will see you clearly. As time goes on, the mother learns to anticipate the baby's needs—when it is the time to feed and his time to sleep; and she watches every little progress in the baby's development with amazement. Then one day, the mother is rewarded by a smile and coos, and her joyful experience continues as she discovers every stage of her baby's development.

Bathing and giving massages to the baby is another precious moment of bonding. By the time twelve weeks pass, soon the baby will be ready for sleep training. Specialists on newborn babies are adept at helping mothers train the baby to sleep through the night. When it happens, it is just the time when the mother can finally look forward to a longer sleep for herself.

> Sons are heritage from the Lord, children are a reward from Him.
> (Psalm 127:3)

Sometimes, a mother may find it wearisome to sit there every two or three hours, breastfeeding and doing nothing else. Aside from just bonding with the child, it would be nice to look on this time as an opportunity to pray with the baby for his spiritual nourishment while his physical body is being fed.

Humming a tune or singing softly while the baby is feeding has a very calming effect to both the mother and the baby. This may be a good time to read or a time to plan when to introduce different tastes to your baby's palate in order to prepare him to start on solid food. Your pediatrician can help you decide when the appropriate time to do this is. Sooner or later, nursing comes to an end.

CHAPTER 4

Successful 0–18 Months

YOU HAVE WATCHED how your baby developed well, and you may have trained him to sleep through the night. You have introduced variety of tastes and solid food, and you have witnessed how he recovered and maintained a healthy weight. The baby has turned on his side, had tummy times, and he smiled and cooed to your great enjoyment. Then he showed signs of teething and attempted to try his strength. He crawled and enjoyed jumping on your lap. He has learned how to call your attention by making noise or crying. Every baby is different, as you might discover, and their rate of development varies from one another. It doesn't matter if the child is your first or second or third. You still learn something new with each one as they develop.

You tell your one-year-old baby to wipe his mouth, and he does just that. He recognizes faces of people in the household and knows his toys. If your child understands and follows concrete commands and learns a sense of ownership, you might want to ask yourself what else he is learning.

It is important for the parents to understand that at this stage, the child is reacting to the world around him through his senses and his experience with the immediate members of the family. Through observation of consistent daily repetition of activities and the quality of interaction with people around him, the child keeps on learning. Parents should bear in mind that the child does not operate by thoughts and ideas, so it is more effective to stimulate his senses by the use of songs and music, rhymes, and the actual experience of nature by taking the child outside for a stroll.

Presuming that the mother has not been successful in consistently including the baby in her daily prayer time, now is the right time to restart. Christian songs and music, picture books, and Bible stories are the best materials to be used in introducing the knowledge about God to this young mind. Explore what God has created to develop the child's appreciation for God so that his concept about a heavenly Father, the creator of all things, becomes concrete.

I remember being trained to kneel with my mother and pray beside her before bedtime and saying grace before or after meals. I still remember part of the very first poem that she taught us to memorize titled "All Things Bright and Beautiful." I grew up at the time when technology was in its infancy, and I am grateful that my mother loved to sing in lieu of radio or television. My mother loves to sing to us, "Jesus loves me, / Jesus loves me, / Jesus loves me, / and the Bible tells me so."

Another favorite action song that we loved to sing in the morning is found in the book of Isaiah 60. "Arise shine for your light has come, and the glory of the Lord has risen, the glory of the Lord has come, the glory of the Lord has risen upon thee." A timeless favorite that we learned and were also taught in school, to our greatest delight, was, "I Got a Joy, Joy, Joy, Joy Down in My Heart."

I chose to mention these powerful examples because of its ability to create the child's appreciation of the infinite and loving God who created all things bright and beautiful. These songs also promote the child's realization of God's love and the joy in his heart that comes from Jesus. There are a lot of beautiful and inspirational songs, rhymes, and poems out there; but the parents must always pay attention to the value of such in the development of child's self-confidence and self-worth, in addition to Christian values.

Whatever the baby learns during the first two years through his intimate interaction with the mother and other members of the family will determine the nature of training in the succeeding years. If the parent has been diligent in incorporating Christian values as early as the first few months of birth, guided by the understanding of the stages of development and learning abilities of a newborn and of a toddler and later as young child, the teaching then becomes a spontaneous process.

CHAPTER 5

Your Child's Emotional Development and You (Two to Seven Years)

> *Train up the child in the way he should go and when he is old he will not depart from it.*
>
> —Proverbs 22:6

IN EVERY DEVELOPMENTAL stage in the life of a child, he wrestles with new skills and new abilities. The age between two to seven years is the time a child goes through a period of intense struggle until he attains mastery. Each breakthrough brings him more confidence. Notice that a child who has made his first few steps is no longer interested in crawling. Once he has learned to hold a spoon, he wants to be independent and no longer wants to be fed. Children love the feeling of mastery, and parents should be there as cheerers and to share in the child's victory.

The act of appreciating the child's victories motivates him to keep moving forward and strive for greater mastery. This builds his self-confidence and makes him appreciate his own abilities. The child's desire for independence continues as he learns new skills. At this stage, the inexperienced and impulsive parent will complicate the child's drive for greater independence.

Toddlers find sharing to be emotionally difficult. Learning to share is a universal problem for parents for children at this age. The truth is, the child is moving from infancy to being independent. They learn to assert themselves and are impulsive. They lack empathy and can grab toys and shove other toddlers without any thought. At this stage, the child is genuinely surprised when the other toddler cries after he grabs the toy.

Gentle reminders help the child learn to think and weigh things before acting. By saying, "That really hurts her feelings when you grab her toy," slowly, the child develops awareness of other people's feelings. Children learn to share from other children in their own way, and parents must be there to show appreciation of the child's acts of gentleness and generosity toward others.

> All Scripture is God-breathed and is useful for teaching, correcting, and training in righteousness. (2 Timothy 3:16)

It has to be noted that the child does not know his limits, nor does he know what is good for him and what is not. However, there is one thing they know; they don't want you hovering over them. It is at this stage that parents have to say no from time to time. Children are confused whenever they hear no since they still do not understand it is to protect them. Each time children don't get what they want, they become frustrated and, most of the time, they go into tantrums. They see parents as hindrances between them and what they want, and this requires patience and understanding. Every healthy child goes through this stage in which they begin to define themselves. This becomes a challenge to the parents themselves as to how to navigate in this crucial period of child's process of maturity. Some parents have learned some effective way of diverting the child's attention into something safer and interesting.

Another thing true at this stage is that children are concrete in their way of thinking and may find abstract ideas confusing. The principle of show and tell is very much applicable to this age group and is highly recommended when teaching concrete activity. This same principle applies when teaching your child how to worship. It is during this time that instilling Christian values has to be demonstrated with increasing emphasis. Children learn from repetitive activity.

If the mother has implemented a structure for the baby from earliest months of birth through a consistent schedule of prayer time following a moment of silence, this has already become part of the child's routine. All the mother needs to do is build on that environment of worship. Picture books and Bible stories should supplement the training, and easy songs of worship that a child can easily follow are the best way to guide the child in Christian living.

> Be joyful always; pray continually; give thanks in all circumstances, for this is the will of God for you in Christ Jesus. (1 Thessalonians 5:16–18)

Remember that the child learns not only by what they hear from their parents but also, most importantly, by what they see. How you practice your faith, how you live, and how you react to various situations has more impact on the child's emotional growth and character development. Allow the child to develop good mental dispositions by asking questions. Ask about their preferences, about their feelings, and about their likes and dislikes. Ask for their opinions on things or activities they are engaged in. Encourage them to make decisions. How you interact with your child in this most crucial part of growing up speaks a lot about you and the kind of parenting you received during your own childhood.

> Let us discern for ourselves what is right; let us learn together what is good. (Job 34:4)

Also important to consider is that your child has his own wants and needs separate from their parents. Too many restrictions cause children to become too compliant with their parents, thereby lacking in self-confidence and self-definition. On the other hand, his frustrations may also lead him to rebel against restrictions. To avoid this, parents must learn the art of diverting the child's attention.

CHAPTER 6

Christian Upbringing

I have no greater joy than to hear that my children are walking in the truth.
—3 John 4

AS PARENTS, IT is our desire to bring into the world delightful children that grow up into admirable adults. This, however, takes a lot of effort and deep concerns for parents. As we strive toward this desire, we encounter testing moments, and we oftentimes deal with our child's tantrums. We grew up in the world of diverse culture that did not offer training in parenting, so we are presumed to learn as we go as ducks are to the water.

I have discussed in previous chapters the importance of instilling our religious practices to the young child as early as possible. This may sound redundant, but the modern way of parenting that is widely accepted in the Western world has far departed from the teachings in the Bible. In fact, the old adage taken from Proverbs 13:24 that says "Spare the rod and spoil the child" is now regarded as unenlightened and medieval style. By this, I do not in any way prescribe physical punishment; but instead, parents must be unyielding when establishing rules and boundaries that children must observe and adhere to.

Whereas modern parenting may work to some extent, it has pits and falls that often result to parents and children at war with each other, and some parents become bullied by their own children. Parents who end up this way are bewildered at how their adorable children turned into bullies and, eventually, went out of control. You try to remain optimistic and positive, hoping this phase will soon pass. The truth is, you really have no idea what to do.

Conscientious Christian parents must turn to the Bible at all times. "Train up the child in the way he should go and when he is old he will not depart from it" (Proverbs 22:6). This verse tells us that we must train the child, and secondly, we must train the child in the way he should go, not in the way we want him to go. This means we must train the child in the way God wants him to go, which I will discuss further later in this section. The second part of this verse assures parents of some peace of mind that as the child grows, his learning will guide him once he goes out into the world and that he will not depart from it.

From here onward, the most important thing that parents should teach children is faith in God. You have taught him the existence of a loving heavenly Father who created all things and provides all things that we are grateful for every day, in every meal, and in every blessing. You have taught him to sing praises and the importance of praying daily, and you included him in your religious practices by taking him to church to attend services. There is a lot to learn from the book *Five Principles of Prayer* written by Rev. Roel C. Tiongco. The book teaches the right way of praying as Jesus himself taught us to pray as it is written in the book of Luke 11, beginning in verse 2.

Now is the time to build his faith and trust in this loving God. In the New Testament book of Hebrews chapter 11, find stories of faith beginning from verse 1 through the last verse. There are verses that give assurance to those who trust in the Word. "Trust in the Lord with all your heart and lean not in your own understanding. In all your ways acknowledge Him and He will make your path straight" (Proverbs 3:5-6). This verse also tells us that God's thoughts are higher than our thoughts; therefore, we must put our trust in Him. If we trust Him over our own understanding and if we acknowledge Him in everything we do, there is a promise in this verse. He will make our path straight. Acknowledging Him will remove all obstacles and hindrances before us. This truth to be learned by a child is so valuable in guiding him until adulthood.

CHAPTER 7

Teaching Obedience

ANOTHER VIRTUE THAT children must learn is obedience. Even Jesus demonstrated obedience as written in John 6:38. He said, "For I have come down from heaven not to do my will but to do the will of him who sent me."

It is understood that while parenting should be a joyous experience, there are anxieties that parents usually had to deal with. There are monetary challenges and time management difficulty, and there may be some health issues that need to be given attention. All these put a lot of pressure on the parents.

Meanwhile, the child continues to master new skills, and with mastery comes the desire for greater independence. He feels stronger and more confident, but it is impossible to be a good parent without saying no to a child from time to time. Here begins the battle of wills.

> Whoever loves discipline loves knowledge, but he who hates correction is stupid. (Proverbs 12:1)

I remember the first day I brought my son to kindergarten. He was so scared to be left alone and wouldn't let go of my hand while screaming. For a few days, the principal allowed me to sit nearby where my son could see me. Days passed, and he became used to be in the class and seemed not to mind not seeing me around anymore. Slowly, the child learns independence.

They learn to express themselves and make their own choices and wants. They will try to get their own way, and this usually leads to conflicts. No child wants to hear the word *no*. My three-year-old grandson once said to me, "Grandma, don't say no. Say yes," when I refused to give him what he wanted. It is human nature to feel rebellious anytime one feels restricted.

As parents impose their will on their children, they clash. Every time parents put restrictions, children see it as a testing moment. The child tries screaming to see if the parent will eventually give in. He may try crying to get his way or making a scene to find out if the mother will ultimately surrender. The parents have options: either to stay firm and refuse to concede or give in to the child. Either way, the child pushes the conflict until you hit your tipping point.

> Everyone should be quick to listen, slow to speak and slow to become angry, for a man's anger does not bring about the righteous life that God desires. (James 1:19–20)

You heard what the child is clamoring for; now you try to decide. You stay firm, give in, or bully back. This brings us back to the early years of your parenting style. As I have previously mentioned, the child learns and develops his emotional responses, attitude, and character based on your interaction with each other and what he sees from you and the people around him. All these factors are carried over while he is growing up, and now he is testing how far he can go. We have to accept the reality that parents have good days and bad days too, and from time to time, they also battle within themselves how to react to this child's bullying. They weigh whether to punish, surrender, or negotiate; but all these responses are bound to fail.

> Make a tree good and its fruit will be good, or make a tree bad and its fruit will be bad, for a tree is recognized by its fruit. (Matthew 12:33)

CHAPTER 8

Why Obey?

> *Children, obey your parents in the Lord, for this is right. Honor your father and mother–which is the first commandment with a promise–that it may go well with you and that you may enjoy life on earth.*
>
> –Ephesians 6:1-4

IT IS EVERY parent's desire to see their children grow up and enjoy good and abundant lives. Meditating on this verse will clearly tell us that children are commanded to obey their parents, for this is right. And anyone can tell us this is admirable. It should not be the other way around. Parents should be parents, not slaves meekly running errands at their child's beck and call.

"Honor your father and your mother" is one of the ten commandments of God, and it is there for a reason. First of all, this commandment carries a promise "that it may go well with you and that you may enjoy life on earth." If this is what you desire for your children, you may as well teach obedience.

Secondly, the father is the first figure of authority in the child's eyes. He is the representative of God in his family. He provides every need and protects everyone in his household, so much like our heavenly Father, while a mother provides emotional support to her children. Children who were trained to recognize this truth will honor their parents unconditionally, and therefore, they may enjoy the promises of God.

> A wise son heeds his father's instruction, but a mocker does not listen to rebuke. (Proverbs 13:1)

This verse of the Bible contains instructions meant to be taught to children. It says to pay attention and to listen well, and for children to remember instructions or teachings, they need to hear it over and over again. They learn from what they hear and see over and over again. Remember when, as children, we were told to memorize a poem or a passage in the Bible? We read it over and over again until we memorized it. When in school, we were told to memorize the multiplication table. We recited it over and over again until we committed it to our memory. This is the same principle that applies to whatever teaching we want to inculcate in their tiny minds.

There are many good children's books that teach good moral lessons, obedience, love, and respect that parents can utilize. These resources are helpful in trying to mold our children into God-fearing, delightful, and wholesome human beings. This is the greatest responsibility of parents above all other things that we can provide to our children.

> If a man curses his father and mother, his lamp will be snuffed out in pitch darkness. (Proverbs 20:20)

I've read books about children turning into bullies, and I personally know parents who are victims of their bully children. Everywhere, you can hear little children and teenagers disrespecting and cussing one another and people in general, having no respect for authority or for the elderly. How did this come about? Where did this come from? The worst question being asked is, Who are the parents of these children?

That is the saddest reality of all; parents are ultimately to be blamed. This type of child who grew up without proper guidance is at risk and is living life in pitch darkness. I differ from the opinion of psychologists who regard it natural and necessary for all healthy children to be in a collision course with their parents to define themselves, to identify themselves differently from their parents. Parents and children in a collision course is a contradiction to the purpose of teaching obedience. Children must maintain a respectful attitude, even if they disagree with parents. Self-definition can be achieved without being constantly in collision with parents. If this is happening, it only show much of the parenting style of which the children are used to.

> He who ignores discipline comes to poverty and shame, but whoever heeds correction is honored. (Proverbs 13:18)

CHAPTER 9

The Principle of God's Love

So we have come to know and to believe the love that God has for us. God is love and whoever abides in love abides in God and God abides in Him.
—1 John 4:16

LIKE ANY OTHER child, I was told that God loves me, but I had no idea how to love Him back. I wish I would also have been told that the Holy Spirit, who is in me, is greater than the one who is in the world. I would have been more courageous and more confident when faced with challenges as a teenager. I didn't know because no one showed me early what is written in the Bible and how the Word of God relates to me in my daily life.

> Love the Lord with all your heart, with all your soul and with all your mind. This is the first and greatest commandment. (Matthew 22:37-38)

My nephew, despite his size (which is bigger than any other seven-year-old child in school), is being bullied; but he will never fight back because he believes Jesus is in his heart, and he doesn't want to lose Jesus. Children relate to Jesus in a very special way, and parents should emphasize that loving the

Lord is keeping his command to love one another. They know Jesus is Lord and Savior, and having been taught in their formative years about the love of Jesus, children will never depart from that belief.

> But seek ye first the kingdom of God and his righteousness, and all these shall be added unto you. (Matthew 6:33)

As a child, if I were having trouble, I would go to the people around me. They would give me advice from their viewpoint of the world. I would be told to give up whatever I was struggling with because it was not for me, or I would be advised to fight back or to give in because the other party was stronger. In those instances, I would end up always feeling like a loser, and that is what the enemy wanted me to feel.

In contrast, a child who has been taught to pray and who is used to call on the name of Jesus will not trust anyone else but will seek the Lord. That should be the mind-set of the child who grew up trusting the Lord Jesus Christ. This child will have more confidence and will not worry about how things will unfold. Every person must grow in faith.

In comparison, picture a child who constantly hears parents complaining about what they lack in life, constantly saying what they cannot afford, and always telling the child he cannot do this or that and that he doesn't know better all the time. This has the power to diminish the child's self-confidence and self-worth. His sense of timidity will be carried on throughout his life if there is no positive intervention.

Without the knowledge of the presence of God in life, a person will feel lost, hopeless, and discouraged. As such, the person will be unable to see anything positive in a negative circumstance; therefore, the person will complain about all the unfortunate events in life. All the negativity that the child hears and sees in his daily life makes it impossible to expect positive outcome when he grows up.

If I am the child and I know that Jesus abides in me, I would think and act differently. If I have that knowledge, it would give me boldness and confidence. I would operate from faith. That knowledge changes my perspective in life and will make me confident that I can overcome any adverse circumstance the enemy will lay before me. I will naturally be positive and will look at obstacles as a means of transporting me to a higher level of success. Fear will have no place in my mind, and I will always emerge victorious in my life because of the assurance of the word of God.

> He who fears the Lord has a secure fortress, and for his children it will be a refuge. The fear of the Lord is a fountain of life turning a man from the snares of death. (Proverbs 14:26–27)

CHAPTER 10

Build Your Child for Greatness

> *Listen my sons to a father's instructions; pay attention and gain understanding. I give you sound learning, so do not forsake my teaching.*
> *—Proverbs 4:1–2*

FEAR OF GOD and love, respect, and obedience to parents must be learned early in life to take root in the child's tiny mind. Having been taught at an early age that there is one loving God who is faithful and full of mercy, a child would naturally trust in Him. During his most difficult times, either in school or in his dealing with other children, he can ask God's help in prayer. Before anyone can come to God, he must first believe and trust in Him. This is the foundation of greatness that we parents desire for our children.

Why do children try bullying tactics when they do not get what they want? A common example of this is when a child starts whining and carries on until he elevates it to bullying. Children normally do not like to hear the word *no* if they ask for something.

"You promised. I hate you!" If you as a parent are teaching obedience, giving in to the demand when it has turned into bullying is the worst response. Giving in or negotiating with a bully will validate the action, and the next time, the child will try same tactic since he had proven that it ultimately works. It does not teach the child respect and obedience, nor would any kind of punishment achieve any benefit for both the parent and the child.

> He who guards his lips guards his life, but he who speaks rashly will come to ruin. (Proverbs 13:3)

Attitude is a pattern of behavior learned for a long period of time. If parents allow this bullying behavior to continue unchecked, it will be carried on until the child grows up. Most bullied parents end up victims to the bully they nurtured and developed.

Immediate action is needed to prevent this attitude to continue and to find out what the underlying cause of the behavior is. There are reasons behind the child's frustration. The most common cause could be tiredness or hunger, or it could be feeling of being left out, especially with the arrival of a new baby. School-age children could be having difficulty in school that he is unable to verbalize. Validating the child's feelings could never go wrong, whereas yelling or punishing will only escalate the problem and worsen the bullying back and forth.

Every year, children progress from the time when everybody loves everybody. As they get older, they learn to form small groups. When they reach high school, they undergo feelings of great uncertainty as they move on to another level of development. This is the time when they begin to compete and desire to belong, and later, they get conscious about their status and hierarchy in the group.

Aside from this uncertainty, they face the stress of turning up good grades and high test scores. They worry about being labeled a nerd, a goody-goody, and the list of other scary labels.

> Whoever loves discipline loves knowledge he who hates correction is stupid. (Proverbs 12:1)

Acknowledging the feelings on display assures the child that he got your attention and that you care for him. This method usually calms down the child and makes him more receptive. Encourage him to talk about his feelings, and he will learn to communicate maturely. Give him praise for being able to discuss it with you without whining or getting into fits of rage.

Parents should encourage children to verbalize their feelings in a respectable and acceptable manner. Let the child see clearly what is bothering him, and allow him to participate in making good decisions for himself with the help of the parents. By offering the best options, your child will learn to process new ideas and new solutions to situations he finds challenging. Help him see the cause for his actions and the effect or outcome that may result from such an action. By consistently going in this particular route, the child develops maturity, and he develops his reasoning ability and the ability to look ahead and beyond the challenge at hand. They then develop and grow to become emotionally matured individuals with admirable character.

> Pride only breeds quarrels, but wisdom is found in those who take advice. (Proverbs 13:10)

CHAPTER II

Framework for Healthy Habits

All your children shall be taught by the Lord and great shall be the place of your children.

–Isaiah 54:13

PARENTING IS PROBABLY the most challenging job in the world. Whatever type of parenting one decides to have has effects that ripple into the child's future and eventually affect the community where he may belong. The social problems arising in every community all over this country can always be traced back to a family.

Aside from giving them the right moral foundation, starting from cradle, it is important that they are healthy and active to make them feel better about themselves. For any sign of frustration that leads to whining, this behavior should not be ignored or minimized. It is always advisable to find out the cause of their frustration at the earliest stage. Help them express their feelings and verbalize their insecurities. Being able to do this is a means for them to achieve emotional growth. It gives them confidence that you are there when you are needed. Show children appreciation every time they overcome their pain.

Encourage them to engage in activities like sports, pursue their talents, or have some hobbies. Keeping them active builds self-esteem and produces personal pride. Children long to be appreciated for their accomplishment. Praise and acknowledge it. Probably the most important component in early training is for parents to establish a consistent structure that must be followed, like time management. Set a time for bed, time for meals, time for homework, and time to do chores.

I came across a posting in Facebook that said a child who is given chores to do at home grows up having sense of responsibility. They learn to value time and effort and show respect for others who are doing their job. There is some truth to this as we can look back to the past generation when children were expected to do chores at home. When they grow up, this type of individuals strive to accomplish meaningful goals in life.

> He who heeds discipline shows the way of life but whoever ignores correction leads others astray. (Proverbs 10:17)

Aside from promoting healthy habits in children, another area that should be given great emphasis is setting limits based on the family culture. Families who are strict on respect and personal responsibility generally do not have bullying issues at home. In contrast, families who are too permissive in parenting style and who fail to provide limits are bound to have children who grow impulsive and unmanageable. Parents wonder where they went wrong.

Setting boundaries is equally important to teach children respect for other people's physical space and respect for other people's feelings. Children must learn to communicate thoughtfully. Parents who are putting into practice the aforementioned framework provide the environment for children to grow into wholesome persons and respectful and God-fearing individuals.

> Commit to the Lord whatever you do and your plans will succeed. (Proverbs 16:3)

Poor structure, without imposed limits, and an absence of set boundaries can build bullying behavior in children. Lack of training in biblical teachings while growing up results in kids uninterested in anything related to God and religious practice. Their concept of right and wrong is always based on their selfish desires. As a consequence, children reflect the culture of the family that raised them.

> To have a fool for a son brings grief; there is no joy for the father of a fool. (Proverbs 17:21)

We can almost always find young people who come to church merely to concede and appease their parents and to avoid altercation. Some come to church and can barely wait to leave as soon as possible. They eventually disappear from the scene, and the longer they stay away from church, the further they go astray. Parents in this situation wonder how this happened, and most of the time, they don't know what to do. It becomes the cause of upheaval at home, and blame goes back and forth.

When we look at this problem closely, it really goes back to parenting style. Abusive parents mostly have an abusive childhood. Permissive parenting style rarely results in positive behavior in children; whereas strict parenting mostly results in a well-mannered and adorable person.

CHAPTER 12

Preteens' Challenges

He who ignores discipline comes to poverty and shame, but whoever heeds correction is honored.

–Proverbs 13:18

LET ME STRESS a very important point that I have previously mentioned: kids' learning paces vary. If it is not met by the school's one-size-fits-all approach, we see kids under tremendous stress. Just as parenting is not a one-size-fits-all method, parents and teachers must understand that each individual child has his own learning style.

Once a child is not performing well in academics, parents usually make a mistake of putting more pressure on the already highly pressured kid at school. Parents should understand that difficulty in keeping up in school is causing the child to feel pressure; thus, he shows changes in behavior–from a happy and friendly kid into an unhappy introvert.

> When I was a child, I talked like a child I thought like a child, I reasoned like a child. When I became a man, I put childish ways behind me. (1 Corinthians 13:11)

This change in behavior may also be exhibited in the form of defiance and bullying. Parents, instead of adding pressure and bullying back, must help kids to channel defiance into a positive outlet to build their confidence and creativity. Parents should be there to guide and allow children to make choices and process different options reasonably. Let them come to a positive solution to the challenges they are confronted with. You want your kid to develop his own opinions and views as he grows into maturity and independence without going beyond the bounds of decent expressions of respect.

Pressure may result not only from the growing schoolwork and more complicated assignments. It may also come from interactions with other children and their peers. When the child feels rejection or when they are being undervalued, they become defiant, and parents must be quick to recognize this symptom. In some cases, children do not necessarily tell parents the complete story about the problem. Parents, in this case, have only partial information. Oftentimes, it can be an unrecognized and concealed feeling of insecurities.

Some children suffer from constant neediness. These are anxious kids who have not learned to be self-reliant and are unable to find their own way in the outside world. They are too fearful of anything unfamiliar or anything new. Parents are unaware that they are the enabler of this anxious bully, thereby causing the child to miss out on many opportunities for growth.

If the child is showing signs of anxiety, there are factors that need to be considered. If the child has always been anxious, one has to look back if there is history of anxiety in the family; therefore, professional help is needed in the scope of mental health. Did the child ever experience a traumatic event in the family? In which case, a more sympathetic understanding must be exercised.

When I was diagnosed with breast cancer and went through the horrible experience of the treatment, I saw my four children dealing with this traumatic event differently. While the two older boys had better resilience, being able to talk to friends, the two younger ones were handling it with more difficulty. Despite their silence I saw their performance in school abruptly impacted. Their grades suddenly plummeted, and no amount of encouragement made any difference. I told them, "That's fine. Seventy-five is passing," just to lift some pressure they were going through. I allowed them to weather this traumatic event on their own, but I constantly assured them that I would be well soon. This somehow eased up their worry until we all overcame this event successfully.

> A fool finds no pleasure in understanding but delights in airing his own opinions. (Proverbs 18:2)

If the anxious behavior happened suddenly, the parent has to examine what is happening presently in this child's life. Changes such as moving to a new home, requiring a change of school or starting a new class and forming new group of friends, all of these can contribute to a feeling of anxiety in children. Children may want to control the environment and everyone in it. They resort to lying, making phony illnesses to manipulate their parents just to manage their own fears and insecurities.

Another angle to look into is age. Developmental shifts happen as soon as kids approach adolescence due to surge of growth hormones. Considering all these factors that I mentioned above, try to get to the root of the change of behavior in order to find a better and easier route to resolve the problem more positively.

> And we know that in all things God works for the good of those who love Him, who have been called according to His purpose. (Romans 8:28)

CHAPTER 13

Developing Social Skills

He who walks with the wise grows wise, but a companion of fools suffers harm.

–Proverbs 13:20

WE HAVE DISCUSSED previously that the most difficult time in a child's life is during middle and high school. This is the time when stress is very high due to growing schoolwork and complicated assignments. This is also the time when they become conscious about who is going with whom and the desire to belong to the most popular group is very high. Their social skills determine whether they gain acceptance or be rejected. At this period, children face complex interactions with parents, teachers, friends, and the group as a whole. They face every aspect of the system and react according to the values and culture ingrained in their own personality. This is when early training comes into play.

Is he aggressive, or is he tempered? Has he gained confidence in himself? Is he considerate and respectful? On the other hand, if he is timid, insecure, lacking in social skills, and unable to relate positively with other children, the child suffers pain as a result. They need help in developing social skills by introducing them to new friends and new groups that can enhance their self-confidence. Encourage them to participate in various activities that build self-confidence.

Parents tend to be biased in their views when watching children interact. As a rule, parents intervene only if necessary but should not worry unnecessarily. Realize that much of the child's sufferings are normal pains that every child experiences during the process of growing up. Adult intervention usually interferes with children working it out on their own. The fact is that as toddlers, they learn from other toddlers. They learn to share through gentle reminders of the importance of sharing. They begin to figure out that by not sharing, they could lose friendship, and from here on, they begin to develop maturity. It is at that stage that they learn how to form and keep friendship.

> An unfriendly man pursues selfish ends; he defies all sound judgment. (Proverbs 18:1)

Concerns are very different with children at risk. They exhibit mean attitude and therefore rarely have real friends and, oftentimes, become the scapegoat for a group. They feel rejected and neglected and become defensive and turn aggressive. Parents must be quick to correct the aggressive behavior before it becomes unmanageable. These children are at risk of dropping out of school. Without proper guidance out in the world, they are at the mercy of the bad elements. They can easily be lured into drug and alcohol, and worse, they can be drawn into criminal activities.

Some of these children become confused and feel hopelessly entangled with the wrong crowd. Failing to get away from the unwanted choice, they fall into depression, and the most vulnerable ones commit suicide. Dealing with children at risk becomes more challenging for parents and teachers in school. Permissive parenting without a proper structure children have to follow produces individuals who are impulsive with an unmanageable character. I cannot emphasize any better the importance of early childhood training. The only solution is to go back to the basics.

Validate their feelings, and find out the cause of their negative behavior. The hands-off or "kids do that kind of thing" approach will fail at this juncture. Another failed style of approach is parents engaging in serious talks and punishments, trying to wrestle with the negative behavior that should have been avoided through proper training in the earlier years.

Parents should be able to replace negative group dynamics with something positive. Our job as parents is to bear their pains with them and also to put it in perspective. Encourage them to verbalize their feelings in a mature way. Appreciate the effort of being able to communicate their concerns. Adults must talk about kindness and compassion without pushing the child into the defensive. Accusing him of the misbehavior will only elevate the conversation into bullying. Instead, parents should encourage him to arrive to a positive idea and solution to the challenges he is facing. Find a way to teach good leadership and conflict resolution skills. Talk about good morality, and never look at your child as a lost cause.

> Dear friend, do not imitate what is evil but what is good. Anyone who does what is good is from God. Anyone who does what is evil has not seen God. (3 John 11)

High school days are such a dynamic period in a child's life. The interplay between friendships and group life becomes complicated. From having close, friendly relationships in middle school, the child's entry to high school is full of uncertainty. At this time, the child feels fearful and realizes he or she is no longer at the top of the heap. Things have changed, new personalities have come into the mix, and group affiliations must be carefully considered. Everyone is changing at a different rate and at a different point. This is a new arena, and in the beginning, you just want to fit in. Then you start to figure out who you really are. As you grow up, you begin to look inward and appreciate your own personal traits.

It is the time when children discover his or her personal power over others. Are they really interested of being bullies? The answer is no. What they really aspire to at this age is to gain power over others. One's place in a group becomes important, and his or her position in the hierarchy is equally important. Being popular requires having good grades and high test scores. It places great demands on how one looks and the family status in the community, and all of these put a great pressure on each child. It pushes the children to either be fake or be real.

Those who succeed at this age are only those with strong self-worth and self-confidence learned from early childhood and who are guided by solid and good family values. They are not threatened by outside influences. They trust in their faith in God, trust their family, and trust themselves.

CHAPTER 14

Cultivating Good Friendship Skills

EVERY CHILD HAS a desire to have a friend as he or she is growing up. From the moment a parent arranges the first playdate for her toddler, the child learns that there are other kids out there that he or she wants to play with. It is the parent's responsibility to lay the groundwork and to provide guidance to this little individual from the choice of crowd to teaching them how to cooperate and share with friends and enjoy the company of others. Teach them how to take turns and control their emotions. It is during this stage of development that children learn the ability to control aggressive impulses. This is the time they develop good friendship skills. Let us not overlook the need to teach children humility.

> Make sure that nobody pays back wrong for wrong, but always to be kind to each other and to everyone else. (1 Thessalonians 5:15)

I keep going back to the time when we must diligently teach and guide our children because of the great impact of their early childhood training on their future behavior and the kind of interaction they will encounter with other children during their growing-up years until adulthood. When we are there to soothe the child when he becomes upset from a lively play, kiss their scratched knee and give a hug to assure him it will be all right. As we respond to the kid's every need, they develop a special attachment to us. We are the home they can come back to between their explorations. Their early attachment to us parents is an important factor in their ability to develop friendships later in life.

Think about the times you comforted your child and the times you cheered his accomplishments. These are the moments that build strong attachment that are necessary in developing friendship skills. In fact, we can safely say that good friendships are a good determinant of adult happiness, and good attachment leads to good peer relationships.

As they continue to mature, they develop the ability to tolerate frustrations, read emotions, solve friendship problems, and have a capacity for reciprocity. They become realistic and gain positive expectations that allow them to approach the world with confidence. Children learn empathy from a parent being empathic with them. When a child's early parenting is consistent and has good attachment, it will help the child manage frustrations and conflicts without drowning in anger and sorrow that are bound to be experienced by any kid growing in maturity.

> The Lord sustains the humble but casts the wicked to the ground.
> (Psalm 147:6)

On the other hand, kids who had not developed good early attachment tend to be anxious and clingy. They are usually withdrawn, angry, and resentful. Sadly, these children are difficult to attach to, and they resist any form of contact. Friendship takes practice, and these skills are built on interactions between children and their trusted adult and, later, between children and their peers.

As soon as the child goes off to college, he or she again forms new friendships, and as much as you made yourself a place your baby can come home to, make your home a place where your child wants to bring his or her friends to. Their social skills and ability to keep friendship last will determine future happiness. In other words, the basic requirement to have the skill to maintain friendship results from the confidence that parents give babies that they are good and appreciated and that they are in good hands.

The Bible teaches in Ephesians 6:1–4, "Children, obey your parents in the Lord, for this is right. Honor your father and mother–which is the first commandment with a promise–that it may go well with you and that you may enjoy life on earth. Fathers, do not exasperate your children; instead bring them up in the training and instruction of the Lord."

Visit NancyStantonBooks.com. For inquiries, email nstantonbooks54@gmail.com.

The other books by the author are
Asdahlia: Child of the Sea (fiction) and *Enchanted Ruler of Pitogo* (fiction).

Printed in the USA
CPSIA information can be obtained
at www.ICGtesting.com
LVHW091551010224
770661LV00005B/102